Matador
9 De Montfort Mews
Leicester LE1 7FW, UK
Tel: (+44) 116 255 9311 / 9312
Email: books@troubador.co.uk
Web: www.troubador.co.uk/matador

ISBN 978-1906221-409

Printed in the UK by Martins the Printers, Berwick-upon-Tweed, UK

Matador is an imprint of Troubador Publishing Ltd

Gasholder 8 with Culross Buildings in the distance *2002*

RAILWAY LANDS

Catching St Pancras and King's Cross

Photographs, text and poems by Angela Inglis
Book design by Nigel Buckner

Cover: St Pancras Railway Bridge with Gasholders *1999*
Dedication page: Gasholders seen from Camley Street Natural Park *1997*

TO

Anthony, Bill, Bruce, Carole,
Del, Dinesh, Hilary, Jasper, Judith, Kate, Lisa,
Malcolm, Michael, Mick, Mike, Nigel, Pat, Peter,
Richard, Rob and Ted

LEGEND

A Granary
B Eastern Coal Drops
C Coal and Fish Offices
D Camley Street Natural Park
E St Pancras Church and Gardens
F Shops in arches of old Coal Depôt
G Western Coal Drops
H Southern Coal Drops
J Gasholders
K Railway bridge over Pancras Road
M Culross Buildings
N Stanley Buildings
O German Gymnasium
P Shops in arches on Pancras Road
Q King's Cross Station
R St Pancras Station and Chambers
S Great Northern Hotel
T British Library

MAP 1
1999 : Before the building of St Pancras International

© A.M.J.L.Delarue 2007

MAP 1
fold-out map

ABOUT THE FOLD-OUT MAPS

Two fold-out maps have been provided, one at the beginning and one at the end of the book. MAP 1 at the beginning shows the King's Cross area in 1999 before the extension of St Pancras Station for the Channel Tunnel Rail Link. MAP 2 at the end shows the area in 2005 after the construction.

Fold out the maps when using the book to identify the location of the photographs. These maps will also help in appreciating the many changes that have transformed the area.

Contents

Foreword

MICHAEL EDWARDS
The Bartlett School of Architecture and Planning
University College London

King's Cross and St Pancras, like all major railway stations, have very distinctive features: immense constructions whose scale often dwarfs their surroundings, torrents of passengers and, for a century, freight surging through the neighbourhood. Such stations are important in the daily lives of commuters and railway workers and in unforgettable moments for arriving migrants, departing soldiers and enchanted tourists. The buildings range from awesome symbols of national unity as in Italy to icons of corporate and civic pride as in Victorian industrial Britain.

Through the twentieth century stations across Europe were in a time warp with little investment and minimal change, though the railways were still major centres of employment in handling goods and moving mail and newspapers. Now, change is widespread and intense as train services are modernised. Where France has led the way with better trains, Britain is

9

in the vanguard of making profits from commercial development at stations. Airports and major stations can be like sponges absorbing money, and King's Cross St Pancras is entering that phase. Much of the resultant profit is being used by HM Treasury to reduce the subsidy needed by the private consortium building and operating the international railway.

In these first years of the twenty-first century a great deal of the seamless ensemble of Victorian transport landscape has been destroyed and, as this book goes to press, many more historic elements are threatened. Though the reconstruction of St Pancras Station has been loyal to Barlow's original, expansive vision, the hinterland may be decimated by the time this book appears. Within a few years we may have more islets of surviving 'heritage' surrounded by a sea of towering slabs.

Station neighbourhoods often have political resilience. Their traditional industries were, and still are, strongly unionised, and St Pancras voters elected progressive councillors. They opposed councils at other times: in the St Pancras Rent Strike of 1960 and in the 80s and 90s by challenging rapacious development, fighting for true 'regeneration' and affirming the community's heritage. Concern for that heritage today is widely shared and actively expressed by all sections of the community.

This is also a site of intense housing pressure, where open-market rents can be ten times those affordable by people earning the minimum wage. Sociologist Ruth Glass, in researching housing east of the railway stations in the 1960s, coined the term 'gentrification' to describe the process she observed of well-heeled high earners displacing working class residents. The word is now in worldwide use, and the social process remains rampant even where it was first named.

Photographer Angela Inglis shares her love and understanding of the exceptional fabric which our community has produced here. These restless acres are both a global interchange for millions in transit, and the precious locale of its passionate people, some long-settled and others just arrived.

1

London Heritage

Old St Pancras Church Gardens in a snowfall, December 1986. Dilapidated tombs with barely legible names. Through the gardens railings, seven gasholders in the distance. I am drawn to them. I walk through the gardens, turn right into Camley Street and enter Dickensian gloom beneath a rusting railway bridge where pigeon droppings fall onto sodden pavements. At the far end of the bridge, behind a high brick wall crowned with barbed wire are the gasholders, massive circular structures which frame the changing sky.

Beyond them, along Goods Way and north of the Regent's Canal stand remarkable brick buildings which have already survived the threat of two development plans: the Granary, the Coal and Fish Offices, warehouses and transit sheds. They do not obstruct the sun and the area is bathed in light, which intensifies the red in the fretted framework of the gasholders and the variegated rust, yellow and grey in the brickwork of the industrial buildings. It is a combination of this light and the railway history attached to this land that sets me on a photographic exploration.

Beside the Regent's Canal is Camley Street Natural Park laid out in 1983 on the site of an old coal drop. This haven, run by the London Wildlife Trust, is ingeniously landscaped to include views over the canal, making it seem larger that its two acres. Here I see the industrial landscape from a different perspective, it rises as harmoniously and naturally as the trees.

When the plans were submitted for the building of the new terminal at St Pancras Station for the Channel Tunnel Rail Link, I foresaw the loss of much of this landscape and photographed it urgently. Its buildings are architecturally interesting: some are gems; they represent a proud and innovative past.

The completion of St Pancras International scheduled for November 14th, 2007, precedes King's Cross Central, the biggest development in Western Europe - sixty-seven acres known as The Railway Lands, rich in a legacy from nineteenth century Britain, whose industry, particularly railways, led the world. How will the sixty-seven acres of King's Cross Central be treated? Will the complex of industrial buildings, canal and filigreed gasholders remain in sufficient focus or will they be swallowed by the new surroundings?

Old St Pancras Church Gardens
May 2000

View of St Pancras Gardens showing the Rhodes family tomb and seven gasholders beyond the iron railings. The Rhodes tomb is still there but by February 2002 all the gasholders except Gasholder 8 had gone. The railings around the churchyard have been replaced with a high brick wall.

Pancras Road and railway bridge
May 2000
Until February 2002 this was a familiar sight with the gasholders rising above the coal drops, the latter once arched cavernous storage spaces for coal from where it was distributed. The railway ran above them. The yellow doors were a storage business. These walls, coal drops and railway bridge were all demolished by June 2004.

1. Rubbed and gauged brick blind arch with yellow stock brick surrounding
2. Area of uncleaned multi stock brickwork
3. Ketton stone decorative corbel bracket on North West Tower
4. Detail of rubbed and gauged brick arch showing the fineness of the joints
5. Detailed area with small Lancet arch arcade and Florentine arches below
6. Cleaned yellow stock brickwork
7. Section of west side buildings new walls rubbed and gauged brickwork
8. Blind arch infill of basket weave brickwork with gauged joints
9. Recessed panel constructed in red facing bricks

1. East side buildings Stiff-leaf carved on impost freize from Ancaster Hard white stone

2. Brickwork corbel detail red facing brick over multi-stock brick wall

3. Red facing brick pilaster on yellow stock brick wall

4. Cleaned yellow stock brickwork

5. West Side Buildings restored cinque-feuille window constructed from Ancaster Hard white stone with a rubbed and gauged brick surround

6. Detail of yellow stock brickwork with red facing brick dentils above

7. South façade window constructed from Ancaster Hard white stone and rubbed and gauged brickwork

8. Area of red facing brick wall with Staffordshire (hard) blue brick corner

9. Newly carved replacement Ancaster Hard white stone capital on North West Tower

1. Renovated Barlow Shed roof
2. Rusty discarded support from the Barlow roof
3. Iron support in German Gymnasium
4. Wrought iron Balcony St Pancras Chambers porch
5. Gilded decoration on Old St Pancras Church gates
6. Church gates before 2001 renovation
7. Section of Stanley Buildings South balcony
8. Steel work on the western side of the new Terminal Shed
9. Early roof construction work on new train shed

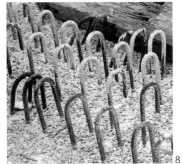

1. Culross Buildings staircase balcony
2. Restored finials on Barlow Shed roof
3. Balcony on window at back of St Pancras Chambers
4. Pinnacle of Old St Pancras Gardens gate
5. Gymnasium window looking out to crane perched on Barlow Shed roof
6. Early construction preparation on new train shed platform
7. Embellishment section of Gasholder 8
8. Gilded decoration on Old St Pancras Church gate
9. Looking up through new train shed at the renovation on the Barlow Shed arch

2

Old St Pancras Church and Gardens

Old St Pancras Church is named after Saint Pancras, a fourteen year old boy beheaded in Rome in 304 AD for his faith. Local historians believe the church was founded ten years later in 314. The church has known periods of disuse during its long history, and of abuse by Cromwell's troops. The appointment of a priest in charge in 1996 re-affirmed it as a regular place of worship. Its fabric and style have been frequently renewed over the centuries.

'The discovery in 1848 of a 6th century altar-stone suggests that the church may have been rebuilt and rededicated at the time of St. Augustine's mission to Britain in 597. There is a 9th century reference to a church here, and the boundaries of the parish may have been fixed then. The building was first mentioned in 1183.' [1] *(See Appendix A1)*

Since the gardens were renovated in 2000-01, faithful to their Victorian style, they are tended daily and are an ideal place for contemplation. The periodic grave breaking by vandals has abated. Today the church is open regularly and the saint's day (12th May) is now celebrated by a Saint Pancras Festival.

Part of the Mission Statement of this parish is *'to seek God's grace in living lives nourished and transformed by the prayer and worship begun on this site nearly seventeen centuries ago and to continue to invite all of his people to be part of it.'* [2]

PHOTOS IN THIS SECTION:

OLD ST PANCRAS CHURCH is set against the snowfall of 2002. On the wrought iron gateway the guilt decoration, recently renewed, catches winter sunlight.

THE SOANE MAUSOLEUM, previously ravaged by time and vandalism, was restored in 1996 by the Soane Monuments Trust, and again in 2000-01 by the London Borough of Camden supported by the Lottery Heritage Fund as part of the restoration of St Pancras Gardens. A plaque erected in 2001 states:

'The Grade 1 listed mausoleum was designed by Sir John Soane, the celebrated architect of the Bank of England (1788-1880), the Dutch Picture Gallery (1811-14) and Holy Trinity Church on Marylebone Road (1824-28).'

The Mausoleum was erected in 1816 following his wife's death in 1815 and bears inscriptions to his wife and second son as well as to himself. A fourth plaque on the north side is left blank on Soane's instruction, marking the fact that he had disowned his first born son who had displeased him.

The plaque continues:

'The "outstandingly interesting monument – extremely Soanesque with all his originality and all his foibles" (Nikolaus Pevsner) bears testimony to the importance of the structure. The central marble cube has four faces for dedicatory inscriptions, enclosed by a marble canopy supported on four Ionic columns. Enclosing this central structure is a stone balustrade with a flight of steps down into the vault itself. The understated classicism of the design is widely seen as one of Soane's most inventive creations and the central domed structure influenced Sir Giles Gilbert Scott's design of the K2 telephone kiosks and subsequent kiosks. It is one of only two Grade 1 listed monuments in London (the other being Karl Marx's tomb in Highgate).'

MARY WOLLSTONECRAFT'S TOMBSTONE, 1797, AS RENOVATED IN 2000. Mary Wollstonecraft was the author of *'A Vindication of the Rights of Woman'*, and the mother of Mary Shelley. Tragically Mary Wollstonecraft died shortly after Mary Shelley's birth.

The original graves of Mary and her husband William Godwin *'were situated in that part of the graveyard taken by the Midland Railway'*. Both she and William were *'removed and re-interred at Bournemouth in a mausoleum belonging to the grandson, Sir Percy Shelley.'* [2]

At some unknown time the tombstone, and not the bodies, was moved to its present position.

THE HARDY TREE *(see page 39)* shows headstones cascading like roots from its trunk. In 1866, when The Midland Railway cut a swathe through St Pancras graveyard, novelist Thomas Hardy was a trainee architect relocating graves for the reburial of corpses. He recorded this experience in a poem:

> *We late-lamented resting here,*
> *Are mixed to human jam,*
> *And each to each exclaims in fear,*
> *"I know not which I am!"*

However, the tombstones around the tree have nothing to do with Hardy's work. They came from the St Gies Cemetery and were left in a dome shaped pile.[3] Later the ash tree seeded itself and grew up through the tombstones moving them upwards as its roots grew larger *(see Appendix A2)*.

In 2003 while land was being excavated on the railway side of the old church wall and railings, more bodies and tombstones were unearthed. A worker alerted the Clergy who caused the work to be delayed till the bodies had been exhumed, re-consecrated and reburied in other burial grounds. According to an article in the Camden New Journal entitled *'Tunnel corpse was French priest'* one of the bodies was the Archbishop of Narbonne, Arthur Richard Dillon. He was *'the son of an Irish Jacobite officer . . . born in France in 1721'* and *'. . . primate of France in 1763.'* He fled during the revolution and died in London in 1806. Recently his *'remains'* were *'reinterred at Narbonne.'*[4]

Three photographs in this section show some of the retrieved tombstones dating back to the 18th century.

1. Camden History Society, Streets of St Pancras, Somers Town and the Railway Lands (page101) published 2002
2. Walter E. Brown, St Pancras Open Spaces and Disused Burial Grounds published by Town Hall, Pancras Road, Camden Town, London 1911 (page 35)
3. Walter E. Brown, St Pancras Open Spaces and Disused Burial Grounds, published by Town Hall, Pancras Road, Camden Town, London, 1911 (page 7)
4. Dan Carrier, Camden New Journal, 5 July 2007 (page 22)

Old St Pancras Church and
wrought iron gilded gates
February 2002
See history above and
in appendix.

32

The Soane Mausoleum
Spring 2002
Erected 1816.
See history above.

The Soane Mausoleum
December 1986
Erected 1816.
See history above.

Old St Pancras Church
and gates
Spring 2006

Mary Wollstonecraft's tombstone, 1797,
as renovated in 2000
April 2001
See history above.

Tombstones

November 2005

Dating back to 18th Century. Found
while digging land for the new railway
lines beside the wall of Old St Pancras
Gardens. More details can be found
in the introduction.

The Hardy Tree
November 2005
See history above and in appendix.

Stacked tombstones
November 2005
Removed during the railway
works ready to be placed
in the Old St Pancras
Church Gardens.

Old St Pancras Church

April 2004

In the distance the new train shed has
taken the place of the gasholders.

Coal Offices

May 2006

The neo-Gothic Coal Offices in Pancras
Road now used as workshops. Once part
of the former Purchese Street coal depot.
They are photographed from
Old St Pancras Gardens.

Tombstones displayed in an S-shape

May 2006

Tombstones taken from land that was a graveyard and now used for the railway. They are paired in an S-shape near to where they were found. See history above.

3

Streets and Stations

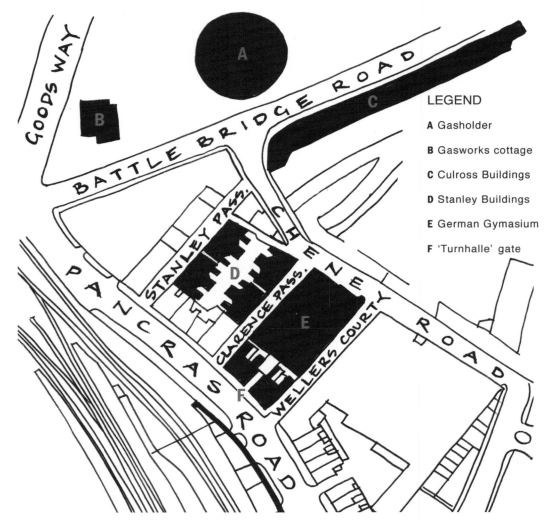

GOODS WAY

BATTLE BRIDGE ROAD

PANCRAS ROAD

STANLEY PASS.

CLARENCE PASS.

CHENEY ROAD

WELLERS COURT

LEGEND

A Gasholder

B Gasworks cottage

C Culross Buildings

D Stanley Buildings

E German Gymasium

F 'Turnhalle' gate

Detail of the area around Stanley Buildings, 1999

3:1. Streets

The photographic section shows CHENEY ROAD LOOKING SOUTH, a narrow street which once extended to King's Cross Station *(see map opposite)*. It is now the new Pancras Road, much widened. In the centre of the photograph is a building with a triangular roof, the German Gymnasium. In WELLERS COURT on the opposite page, its side wall and a metal support are visible. The cobbled street in the picture, now gone, is Wellers Court.

THE GERMAN GYMNASIUM has been restored by London and Continental Railways as an exhibition space. The following photographs show the process of restoration and the front façade after restoration. An interior photograph shows a laminated timber arch supported by an iron spandrel.

The Gymnasium was built in 1864-65 for the German Gymnastic Society, a sporting association established in London in 1861, designed by Edward A. Gruning and constructed by Piper and Wheeler at a cost of £6000.[1] London and Continental Railways call it the 'Gymnasium', and not the 'German Gymnasium', thereby erasing a reference to its historical past. The original entrance on Pancras Road was demolished in February 2002 to make way for the extended platforms and concourse being built at St Pancras Station as part of the Channel Tunnel Rail Link. It is a sad loss.

The original doorway to the German Gymnasium, Turnhalle meaning Gymnasium. Taken from a slide by Malcolm Holmes, 1999.[2]

STANLEY PASSAGE ran from the old Pancras Road to Cheney Road, *(see map above)*. The brick wall abutting Stanley Passage was a vibrant orange rust. On the left were two gasholders, the nearest one has now been demolished, while the other, Gasholder 8, still stands in front of Culross Buildings. It is on the east side of the new Pancras Road. On the right of the photograph is the curved end of Culross Buildings used as offices until 2001. Culross awaits its demise, but the wall has already been demolished. *(See Chapter 6 for more photographs of Culross Buildings).*

BRILL PLACE features in two photographs. This is a recent name suggested in the 1980s by the Borough Archivist, Malcolm Holmes,[3] its old name Phoenix Road being of uncertain origin. The name was adopted in the 1990s. The Brill was originally a farmhouse and later a tavern 'recorded as early as 1690' [4] close to the railway bridge.

The small red brick building with a chimney, marks the place where railway tracks once crossed on a bridge, demolished in the 1980s, to take goods trains into the upper level of the Midland Railway goods depot. This little house was a charming leftover and looked like a miniature cottage. It was demolished in 2002. In the distance is the pink and white St Pancras Railway Bridge.

THE LONG BRICK WALL was once the northern edge of the Midland Railway's goods depot. The Barlow Shed (St Pancras Station) can be seen in the distance. Both the wall and the little house glowed in strong sunlight highlighting the texture of the brickwork.

The BATTLE BRIDGE FLATS were thirties red brick buildings on land between Battle Bridge Road and Goods Way; behind them stood two gasholders and on the north west side the other five. They were designed by John Gower for the British Steelwork Association and demonstrated a particular form of steel construction.

The last five photographs are different views under the ST PANCRAS RAILWAY BRIDGE. The bridge was designed to accommodate the five roads that converged here. It was a photographer's dream for light and shadow.

Everything in the last photograph in this chapter has been demolished. The railway now runs through this area, and Goods Way, the road running ahead no longer exists in that position. It has been re-routed closer to Camley Street Natural Park.

Traffic now travels under the railway at a point higher up in Pancras Road, *(see map 2, After the Building of St Pancras International)*. The new concrete and steel bridge is daunting. It accommodates 15 different railway lines.

---

1. Information from Camden History Society, Streets of St Pancras, Somers Town and the Railway Lands (pages 77-78) published 2002
2. Malcolm Holmes, until February 2007, Senior Archivist, London Borough of Camden Local Studies and Archives
3. As above
4. Camden History Society, Streets of St Pancras, Somers Town and the Railway Lands (page 45) published 2002

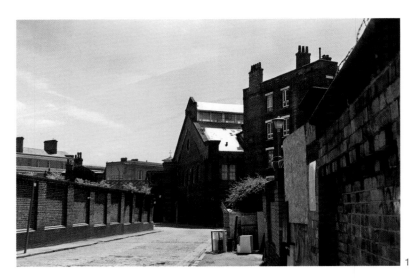

1. Cheney Road looking south
May 2000
The building with the triangular roof is the German Gymnasium built 1864-5. This road is now the new Pancras Road. See maps.

2. Battle Bridge Road
Summer 2000
Walls protecting two gasholders, one being Gasholder 8, demolished by autumn 2001.

1. Wellers Court
May 2000
Side of the German Gymnasium looking onto Cheney Road. The buildings to the right and centre have been demolished.

2. Cheney Road
May 2000
Looking north. Now the new Pancras Road. Gymnasium on left preserved. Wall on right demolished by 2002.

1. Gymnasium undergoing restoration
November 2002
Built 1864-5. See history above.

2. Gymnasium
2005
Showing restoration of the facade. Taken from Barlow Roof.

1. Gymnasium Interior
April 2006
Laminated timber arch supporting an iron spandrel.

2. Gymnasium Interior
April 2006
Decorated iron pillars.

3 Gymnasium Reflections
April 2006

Stanley Pasage running
into Cheney Road
1999
Demolished 2001.
Culross Buildings can be seen to the
right.

58

1. The Little House,
Brill Place
May 2000
Built about 1868. Demolished 2002.
See history above.

2. The Long Brick Wall,
Brill Place
May 2000
Built about 1868. Northern edge of
the Midland Railway's Goods Depot.

1. Battle Bridge Flats
May 2000
Side view from Battle Bridge Road
showing Gasholders and Waterpoint.
Flats built 1936, demolished 2001.

2. St Pancras Railway Bridge
with gasholders
1999
Gasholders dismantled by February
2002. Bridge demolished by June 2004.

1. St Pancras Railway Bridge
May 2000
Built about 1866. Demolished June 2004.

2. St Pancras Railway Bridge
May 2000
Showing the red brick gothic arches in the wall.

1. St Pancras Railway Bridge
May 2000
Looking towards the junction of
Midland Road and Brill Place.

2. St Pancras Railway Bridge
May 2000
View up the old Pancras Road towards
the Gardens of Old St Pancras Church.

St Pancras Railway Bridge
May 2000
Looking towards Goods Way. Nothing in this view remains. Goods Way was re-routed by 2003 and the buildings seen through the bridge demolished by 2002. The bridge was pulled down by June 2004.

Streets and Stations
3:2. Old St Pancras Station

The Barlow Shed, (St Pancras Station) features frequently as part of the photographic landscape. It was *'designed by William Barlow (1812-1902), Engineer in Chief to the Midland Railway, and built between 1866 and 1868, it was and remains an engineering marvel. Wrought-iron lattice arch ribs (originally painted sky blue and all proudly bearing the legend "manufactured by the Butterley Company, Derbyshire 1867") spring from platform level and rise over 100 feet to meet in a slightly pointed apex. They cover what was (in 1868) the largest enclosed space in the world. The shed is 690 feet long and 240 feet wide, and the floor acts as a tie to the arch, a daring concept that had not been attempted before. The tracks were raised 20 feet above the Euston Road so that the trains could run on a level from Camden Town over the River Fleet and the Regent's Canal. The pillared vaults beneath were designed to store Burton beer barrels, a highly lucrative traffic for the Midland Railway, with a hydraulic lift to take the wagons up and down.'* [1]

The first passenger train to run out of St Pancras on 1st October 1868, was the 10am to Manchester, with the first stop at Kentish Town. It then ran non-stop to Leicester, a distance of 97½ miles, at that time the longest non-stop rail journey in the world.[2] The last train out of the Barlow Shed ran on 9th April 2004, Good Friday, leaving at 23.40 for Derby.[3]

The following photographs were taken from 1999 to 2001 just before renovation started on the Barlow Shed, which even then was majestic in its old age.

THE ST PANCRAS WATERPOINT

This was designed by Sir George Gilbert Scott and is a fine example of Victorian Gothic architecture. It was used by the railways to supply water for steam traction. Rather than being destroyed to make way for the new high speed rail link to the Channel Tunnel, it was moved 700 yards to its present position. It dates from 1870 and was part of the complex of buildings making up the station and hotel.[4] *(See Chapter 3:3 for details of hotel)*.

---

1. Camden History Society, Streets of St Pancras, Somers Town and the Railway Lands (page 105) published 2002

2. Malcolm Holmes, Borough Archivist

3. Ken Clench, railway enthusiast

4. Information from pamphlet The St Pancras Waterpoint, available at St Pancras Yacht Basin, Camley Street, King's Cross, London, NW1

Barlow Shed from Midland Road

May 1998

The old coal drops where coal was once desposited for distribution. At the time of this photograph they were being used for garages and small businesses.

1. Pancras Road
Easter 2002
Showing Station Building
before renovation.

2. Pancras Road
Easter 2002
A view further south of the same
building as in photograph 1.

1. The old Barlow Roof
April 2003
Built between 1866-1868.

2. The old St Pancras Station
April 2002
Built between 1866-68.

Barlow Shed

May 2000

A view of the western side before renovation taken from Midland Road showing the craftsmanship of the old building. Built 1866-68.

Barlow Shed
July 2006
Similar view to previous page six years
later. It shows how the wall has been
replaced by glass and steel and the old
arches in Midland Road restored.

73

1. Waterpoint
May 2000
In original position by the railway.
See history above. Built 1870.

2. Waterpoint
Spring 2002
Showing new position in
St Pancras Cruising Club Gardens.

1. Waterpoint
Easter 2004
Seen across the St Pancras Cruising
Club Basin from the Regent's Canal
tow-path. Note its proximity to
the railway.

2. Waterpoint
February 2006
Seen from the railway.

Barlow Shed

Summer 2002

Dismantling the old wall on the
eastern side to make way for the building
of the new extended train shed.

Barlow Shed

October 2004

View from inside the shed looking at the half completed terminal extension on the eastern side. Cecil Rhodes House, The Chenies and the St Pancras Hospital Tower are visible in the distance.

Streets and Stations

3:3. St Pancras Chambers

'Late in 1865 a competition was held to design the station hotel with around 150 bedrooms. Of the eleven architects, Sir George Gilbert Scott (1811-78) submitted a grand plan considerably larger than the original specifications, with more than 300 bedrooms. His was an original design. Any suggestion that the plans had been adapted from those he had submitted for the Foreign Office building in Whitehall is quite wrong, though the story is often repeated.

'Financial problems caused delays in the building of the hotel and the eastern wing of the building was not opened until 5th May 1873, with the rest opening in the spring of 1876. The hotel fabric had cost £304,335, decoration and fittings £49,000, furnishings £84,000, a total of £437,335. Gillow (now Waring and Gillow) were closely involved in providing furniture and furnishings. The completed building had used 60 million bricks and 9,000 tons of ironwork. The polished columns of fourteen different British granites and limestones are frequently mistaken for marble.

'In its heyday, the Midland Grand Hotel was one of the most opulent in London, with over 300 bedrooms. The building had many innovative features including *hydraulic 'ascending rooms', revolving doors and fire-proof floor construction, but it still relied on armies of chambermaids to carry coal and hot water to each of the guest bedrooms.*

'In 1879 a room, breakfast and dinner cost 14 shillings (70p). By 1911 the Baedeker Guide referred to the hotel as having 400 rooms with dinner priced at 5 shillings (25p) and for bed and breakfast 12 shillings (60p). In 1930 prices for rooms started at 8 shillings and 6 pence (42p), with private bath 15 shillings (75p), 4 shillings (20p) for breakfast, 5 shillings (25p) for lunch and 7 shillings and sixpence (37 p) for dinner.

'The hotel closed in 1935; its facilities were outdated and it was too expensive to run and refurbish. It was then used as railway offices and renamed St Pancras Chambers. In the 1960s the building was saved from demolition and given Grade I listed status in recognition of its importance as a great example of high Victorian gothic architecture. In the 1980s the building failed its fire certificate. It was closed down and has been empty until now.'[1]

The restoration of the exterior was completed in 1995 *'at a cost of around 10 million. In June 1996 the building was transferred to London and Continental Railways (LCR), promoters of the Channel Tunnel Rail Link. Following an extensive development competition, LCR selected the Chambers Group as the preferred developer of St Pancras Chambers, which now fronts the new international station at the St Pancras end of the Channel Tunnel Link.'*[2]

This meant that the restoration of both the station and St Pancras Chambers could be completed as part of the same project. It also meant that the hotel would be restored to its former glory with many additional improvements due to modern engineering. It is to be run as a 245-bed 5-star Marriott hotel. Whereas before it was just an hotel, now it will also contain *'68 Manhattan loft apartments'*.[3] It will also accommodate business conferences. The loft apartments have already been sold before completion, so great is the prestige of this location at the gateway to the British Isles.

Much of the original decoration, including the stencilling, mosaics and ornamental ceilings have survived, many behind recent alterations. One of the features of this building is its staircase decorated at the top with paintings of the virtues by Andrew Benjamin Donaldson who worked for Gillow. They have been extensively restored by removing up to seven layers of varnish and accumulated grime. Painted between September 1876 and February 1877 they represent humility, liberality, industry, chastity, temperance, truth charity and patience. In the centre is the first coat of arms of the Midland Railway incorporating features from the arms of some of the cities it served - Birmingham, Derby, Bristol, Leicester, Lincoln and Leeds.[4]

---

1. Malcolm Holmes – Until February 2007 Senior Archivist, Camden Local Studies and Archives
2. Malcolm Holmes as above
3. Channel Tunnel Rail Link – At a Glance pamphlet, produced by LCR
4. Information taken from Malcolm Holme's talk on St Pancras Chambers

St Pancras Chambers
November 2002
Work on the underground was being undertaken in the front of the Chambers.

82

Charity

November 2004

One of the eight Virtues painted from
September 1876 to February 1877 by
Andrew Benjamin Donaldson who
worked for Gillow.

Ceiling Decoration
November 2004
Second floor room.

1. Central Staircase
November 2004

2. Service Lift
November 2004
Fifth floor.

3 Hotel Post Box
November 2004
Ground floor.

1. Archway
October 1994
Porch exit on Euston Road. Note the Ancaster stone and the rubbed engaged brickwork.

2. Entrance to St Pancras Station and Ticket Hall
November 2004

3 Stencilling
November 2004
Wall on first floor leading to the Ladies' Smoking Room.

1. Kitchen Wall in basement
November 2004

2. Gents Toilet with glass tank
November 2004

1. An old door
November 2004

2. Staff Quarters, eighth floor
November 2004
Showing the height and breadth of the
architecture. Tanks and pipes are on
open display.

1. Minton Hollins Tiles
November 2004
In the basement.

2. Minton Hollins Tiles
November 2004
In the basement.

3 Ceiling Stencilling
November 2004
First floor.

Doorway
November 2004

The Ladies' Smoking Room
November 2004

3:4. King's Cross Station and the Great Northern Hotel

KING'S CROSS MONUMENT

We read in an article entitled *'The Man who made King's Cross'* from the Camden History Review 17 that *'the area of London known as King's Cross takes its name from an extraordinary building, erected without any authority by a group of entrepreneurs on land to which they had no title. It stood at an important junction at the meeting of three busy roads now known as Euston, Pentonville and Grays Inn Roads'*,[1] where King's Cross Station is today.

For the first five years of its life this small building, a badly lit traffic hazard in the middle of the road was used as a police station. The statue of George 1V was finally erected on top of the building in 1835, five years after his death, as a *'national monument . . . to be called King's Cross'*.[2] Due to lack of funds it was far from what was envisaged and finally in 1845 it was all knocked down.

Robert Leon writes: *'Such a monument conferred little credit on the architect or the sculptor and did nothing to enhance the area nor the memory of George 1V. Nevertheless, for better or for worse, King's Cross was now complete'*.[3]

Stephen Geary's intention of building such a 'landmark' was to change the name of the area then known as Battle Bridge. (This stems from the legend that a battle took place between Boudicca and the Romans in AD 61 near a bridge over the River Fleet). Battle Bridge had an unsavoury reputation and Stephen Geary had plans to make the area a very different kind of place.

KING'S CROSS STATION

King's Cross Station *'is the oldest surviving railway terminus building in London. Its two semicircular lunettes, (arched windows in a semi-circular space) reflecting the arches of the train shed roofs behind, are separated by a 120 feet high clock tower topped by an Italianate roof. The clock now chiming once more, is by Dent and was exhibited at the Great Exhibition of 1851.'* [4]

The photograph of the train shed from the northern end shows clearly *'the ribs of wrought iron (which in 1866-67 replaced the original laminated timber) rising from dignified brick arcades. The departure and arrival sheds are spanned by two round arched roofs, each with a span of 105 feet, and cover an area*

95

800 feet long, 210 feet wide and 72 feet high. When the station opened on 14th October 1852 it was the largest in Britain, but it soon was unable to cope with the amount of traffic. This increased further after 1857 when the GNR allowed the Midland Railway Company to run into the station, although it was frequently said that Midland trains were deliberately held back to give precedence to those of the GNR. The Midland Railway withdrew after its St Pancras station opened in 1868.' [5]*

Plans have been submitted by Network Rail for restoration of King's Cross Station. The buildings in front of the station are to be removed in order to expose the fine plain brick façade, and to provide a large open space. Local conservation groups are concerned that the façade on the western side of the station should also be seen as originally conceived and that the wrought-iron porte-cochère now in storage, *'formerly the station's main entrance . . . built to protect passengers alighting from carriages',*[6] is restored to its rightful place. At the moment the plans have not included the porte-cochère or the total exposure of the western façade.

There is a glimpse of the Great Northern Hotel on the left of the photograph on the next page. It was added to the station by *'Lewis Cubitt in 1854 and built in a curved plan to follow the original line of Pancras Road, which was later diverted to the west. The exterior has been refurbished, but the hotel was closed in February 2001. It owed its longevity to its simple, hence easily maintained, layout and construction. Cubitt designed the hotel to look inwards (and away from the rather ramshackle terraced houses opposite, demolished in 1871) towards the station across a large garden, which has since been engulfed by extensions to the station.'* [7]

---

1. Robert Leon, The Man Who Made King's Cross, Camden History Review 17 page 13

2. As above (page 14)

3. As above (page 16)

4. Camden History Society, Streets of St Pancras, Somers Town and the Railway Lands (page 74) published 2002

5. As above (page 78)

6. As above (page 78)

7. As above (page 74)

King's Cross Station
August 2004
Seen from Camden Council Offices in Argyle Street showing the
works on the underground and part of the Great Northern Hotel.

King's Cross Station
November 2006
The oldest surviving railway terminus in
London. Its two semicircular lunettes reflect
the arches of the train shed roofs behind.
Built 1851-2.

King's Cross Train Shed, northern end
April 2004
Note the ribs of wrought iron rising from
brick arcades.

King's Cross Station

April 2004

Taken from Goods Way with St Pancras Chambers Tower in the distance. The sheds are spanned by two arched roofs, each with a span of 105ft. They cover an area 800ft long, 210ft wide and 72ft high. Built 1852.

4

Gasholders

Gasholders

The gasholders were built when *'the Imperial Gas Light & Coke Company, formed in 1822, began a new works beside the canal . . . The company ceased to manufacture gas here in 1904; by then there were nine gasholders on the site.'* 1

Parts of their structure date from 1861 onwards, and include several designs with classical embellishments. They were erected by the Imperial Gas Light & Coke Company whose works were built alongside the canal in 1824, so that coal could be delivered and ashes and by-products despatched from a private canal basin. The works distributed gas to different areas of London. The large tanks storing the gas were supported by the holders, and moved up and down as they filled and then emptied.[2]

Professor Germaine Greer, in her article, Cornerstone writes:

'The unadorned gasholder is the elegant realisation of a staggeringly simple concept. The "wet" gasholder develops the principle of a bell inverted in water, which will rise as gas is pumped into it and sink as the gas is removed.

The principle has been understood by engineers for centuries before a man remembered simply as Tate, who is not even recognised by the Dictionary of National Biography, built the first telescopic holder for town gas in 1824. Its purpose was to cushion the fluctuations of demand and supply, as excess gas accumulated during times of low usage only to flow out faster than it could be produced when the gas mantles were lit in streets and houses'.[3]

The three famous gasholders, designed by John Kirkman, joined together by one spine, Listed Grade II, were known as the Gasholder Triplets. Uniquely their circumferences were not tangential to each other but intersected each other. These, together with the other gasholders, were a King's Cross landmark. The sole remaining gasholder, Number 8, standing on its original site at Battle Bridge Road is identical in style and construction to these 'triplets' and is itself listed. The latticed frames around the gasholders were built at a later date. They add to the beauty of their structures. Although the Imperial Gas Company ceased to manufacture gas here in 1904, the gasholders were still in use until 1999.

The Gasholder Triplets were dismantled by February 2002, and are in storage ready to be re-erected as part of the new King's Cross Central development. The developers, Argent (King's Cross) Ltd., propose putting housing inside them. Gasholder 8, which is still standing, is also due to be dismantled and re-erected, its use to be decided later. Germaine Greer prophesies that:

. . . 'we'll miss the gasholders, disappearing all over England, as much as we miss the windmills that used to add focus to the agrarian landscape'.[4]

---

1. Camden History Society, Streets of St Pancras, Somers Town and the Railway Lands (page 89) published 2002

2. Information from the book above and also from Michael Parkes, a town planner

3 & **4.** Germaine Greer, Article Cornerstone, SPAB News, Vol 24, No 4

THE GASHOLDERS - KING'S CROSS

Your makers sculpted you to rise as high
as King's Cross Station's arch. Your circles spun
in air, latticed frames, like eyes above
the Camley Park, Old St Pancras Church,
Culross, Stanley Buildings where Fred Astaire
and Ginger Rogers danced on the wall, barges
afloat on the Regent's Canal, pipes that snaked
your gas away, railway lines, barbed wire
caging you, running wild along brick walls.

I often wandered past to see your wheels
of steel intricately wrought like lace stained pink,
held by annulets, lovers' rings with black
square stones. At evening I watched the sun splash
your pink with red, and conjure your hoops to join,
circling chains twining and intertwining
like dancers in the air. White vapours skimmed
behind your capitals, then disappeared
to leave deep blue sharpening your silhouette.

This was the place for studying skies, where clouds
grew black and pushed your rings so close to earth
you frowned, though, often when the sun broke through
a rainbow ran between your arcs, and made
the raindrops flicker on your metalwork.
But now dismantled, stored away, only one
of you is left, bereft, like Boudicca
who might have met her fate at Battle Bridge,
this ancient place where roads and rivers met.

Angela Inglis   109

Circles in the Air
1999
Shows five gasholders together in Goods Way. Three of these gasholders, the Triplets, were dismantled by February 2002 and put in storage ready to be re-erected on the King's Cross Central development. They will contain housing.

1. Reflection of Gasholders
1997
Camley Street Natural Park pond.

2. Section of Gasholder Triplets by Water Point
May 2000
Water Point Preserved. See history Chapter 3:2.

3 Gasholder Triplets
1997
Taken from Goods Way.

Section of Triplets with barbed wire
May 1999
Taken from Goods Way.

Gasholder Triplet, Goods Way
October 1994
Built about 1861, in use until 1999, dismantled by February 2002. Will be re-erected for housing in the King's Cross Central Development.

Triplets, Goods Way
October 1995

1. Gasholders
Summer 1999
Corner of Goods Way
and Camley Street.

2. Section of Gasholder 8
April 2004
Taken from near Battle Bridge
Road showing embellishments.

Close-up
May 2000
Taken from Goods Way.
Dismantled by February 2002.
To be re-erected for housing
sometime in the future on the
King's Cross Central Development.

Gasholders by Culross Buildings
1999
Seen from the junction of Cheney
Road with Battle Bridge Road. The
nearest Gasholder is now demolished.
Gasholder 8 behind is still standing.
It is to be dismantled and re-erected
on the King's Cross Central
120   Development for community use.

Last of the Triplets
January 2002

Dismantling the Triplets
October 2001
Dismantled by February 2002.

Gasholder 8 on its own
Spring 2002
Goods Way. Still standing, soon to be dismanted and re-erected on new development.

124

Panorama

November 2005

Showing Stanley Buildings' chimneypots, Gasholder 8, Coal and Fish Offices to the left and the Granary to the right, the latter two to be preserved. Gasholder 8 is to be dismantled and re-erected on King's Cross Central Development.

5

Stanley Buildings

Stanley Buildings

Stanley Buildings North and South are the last of five original 5-storey blocks built by the Improved Industrial Dwellings Company in 1864-5, on plans derived by Sydney Herbert Waterlow (1822-1906) and his builder, Matthew Allen, from the Model Dwellings designed by Henry Roberts (1803-76) for the Great Exhibition of 1851. Three Stanley Buildings were lost to wartime bomb damage and to later road alterations.

The IIDC founded in 1863, was one of the earliest philanthropic housing companies attempting to relieve the overcrowding of the poor. Its chairman was Lord Stanley (later Earl of Derby and Prime Minister). Stanley Buildings comprise some of the oldest surviving working-class flats in London and were planned to have private sanitation and good ventilation, very advanced concepts for their time. Each flat had its own scullery and lavatory, and dust and ash chutes ran down the spine of the stairwells. These sturdy and handsome buildings compare very favourably with modern so-called 'affordable' housing, in an area where such housing is desperately short. One of the attractions of these blocks are the cast-iron access balconies served by an open central staircase. The blocks had innovative fireproof floor construction of steel and concrete. No subsequent designs of philanthropic housing were as ornate.

Recent residents recall these buildings with great affection; they felt part of a special community. They made the place their own, and with the help of Graham Nobbs, a gardener, created an oasis in the city centre. Tony Holland, a former resident, recalls a secret garden in an old car park with a wooden stage overgrown with jasmine, with miniature fountains made out of old bath-tubs stacked on top of each other, and where newts and small frogs happily hopped around in the undergrowth.

Graham Crostan, one of the last residents to leave (all of them were forced to move by 2001 due to the development of the new international station) remarked how important such places are and that *'a human in isolation is not a human any more'*.

Mike Leigh set his 1988 film High Hopes here, and many other film companies have used Stanley Buildings, the gasholders and the streets around them as a backdrop. The Ladykillers was filmed in this area. In High Hopes the lead character takes his old mum up to the roof to see the trains pulling out of St Pancras Station. *'It's the top of the world,'* she exclaims.

These buildings were sliced in half to make way for the new Channel Tunnel Rail Link train shed. Stanley Buildings North, a Grade II Listed Building has now been completely demolished in order to straighten the access road to the new St Pancras terminal. There are plans for Stanley Buildings South, also Grade II Listed to be entombed in an eight-storey glass block, trapping the chimney pots, cast iron balconies and distinctive shape of the buildings in a sterile time capsule.

Source: Judith Martin, Projects Organiser, Industrial Buildings Preservation Trust.

STANLEY BUILDINGS NORTH AND SOUTH

Sliced in half
Stanley Buildings
await their fate
some window panes
replaced with ply.

The North is condemned.

The South will be
embedded in glass
eight storeys high.

Ten wrought iron
balconies plead
to passers by;

Look up, look up
let our artistry
raise your eyes
to the roof.
Can't you see
we could be
homes again for you?

Angela Inglis

Stanley Buildings North
May 2000
134   Seen from the old Pancras Road.

1.Stanley Buildings North and Stanley Passage

May 2000

The passage went from old Pancras Road to Cheney Road.

2. Dancers on the Wall

October 1994

A mural of Fred Astaire and Ginger Rogers created in the 1980s. A landmark much loved by the local residents.

Stanley Buildings North
from Cheney Road
May 2000

Stanley Buildings South
from Clarence Passage

May 2000

This half of the building is still standing but
the half out of view was demolished in 2002
to make way for the new train shed.

Balcony

April 2006

Stanley Buildings South, Clarence Passage,
facing the north-western side of the
Gymnasium. Even in its dilapidation
the beauty of the balcony and pillars
are evident. This same balcony is
seen in the previous photograph.

Stanley Buildings
Summer 2002
Ready for the Bulldozer.

Stanley Buildings
September 2002
The two buildings cut in half to
make way for the railway.

Demolition of Stanley Buildings North
June 2007
Stanley Buildings was a Grade II
Listed Building.

6

Culross Buildings

Culross Buildings was built in 1891-2 for the Great Northern Railway to house workers displaced by the building of the new suburban station to the west of King's Cross train shed. It was named after GNR chairman, Lord Colville of Culross KT, who maintained that position from 1880 to1895.

A letter from Richard Johnson, engineer to the Great Northern Railway, to the LCC architects describes how *'as there is a great difficulty in procuring houses in the neighbourhood'*, the new block of buildings has to be completed and the tenants transferred to them before the older dwellings on the site of the new sidings can be demolished. In the light of the way 'improvements' were often made, this is remarkably thoughtful and foresighted.

Like Stanley Buildings, Culross Buildings were an advanced design, and had drying areas on the roof as well as a heating system of warm air through galvanised iron ducts. The flats were reached from open communal stairs with wrought iron balustrades. The method of access was felt to be more humane than the long balcony access of, for example, the early philanthropic flats off Whitechapel Road in East London, where tenants resented the constant monitoring of their movements by the superintendents. There was a basement for railway workshops and mess-rooms, accessible only at the rear from the railway tracks, and a hall. The Culross Hall, which was originally built as a centre for religious guidance and recreation, had a reputation in the early 20th century for political activism. Battle Bridge Road, where the block is located, has the original landscape, but the granite setts have now been removed.

Later Culross, together with the Stanley Buildings (see chapter 5), became a place for short stay housing. Ray Yates, a resident of Stanley Buildings 1991-2001 remembers Culross Buildings very well. He relates how much the people who lived in Culross valued their time there. Graham Nobbs, the gardener mentioned in the previous chapter, helped the residents to create six roof gardens, one for each block. It was an area where plants and small trees grew in pots, where sculptures and murals were displayed, where climbing plants entwined the railings, where coloured lights at night were a permanent feature. There was also a small rooftop pond with goldfish, a built-in barbecue, an entertainment area under a tent and sofas and deckchairs for comfort. It was a place for people to meet and relax, to listen to music, to talk, to admire the sunsets over St Pancras, to look at the skyline and pick out the London landmarks such as St Paul's Cathedral. Ray Yates writes *'Culross roof was the centre of our world'*.

Running east/west across the site where the rail lines all run north/south, Culross Buildings relate to the canal and indicate the layout of the old goods yard, which dictated their position. The windows and doors are now bricked up and Culross is due for demolition to make way for the King's Cross Central development, removing important evidence of the history of the site.

Source: Judith Martin, Projects Organiser, Industrial Buildings Preservation Trust

CULROSS BUILDINGS 1892

wrought iron balustrades
curve like birds' wings
on communal stairs
coloured bricks
pattern the walls

carefully crafted
industrial art

Knock it down
put up shops
business blocks
cafes for the
internet.

Crush the bricks
melt the iron,
but save perhaps
those granite setts.

Old tenement
standing in the way
of shopping malls -

it has to go.

Angela Inglis   149

Chimney Pots at Twilight
October 2004
Culross Buildings.
See history above.

Culross Staircase
November 2004
Showing wrought iron decoration.

Culross Buildings
October 2006
From the eastern end.

1. Derelict Culross
June 2007

2. 150 People Live Here
It is five years since the last person left.
Photo, Michael Edwards.

Window

May 1998

Culross window showing the reflection of
Gasholder 8 and the other gasholder,
that stood with it.

Gasholder 8 and
Culross Buildings
August 2004
In the distance are the top
stories of The Great Northern
Hotel and western façade of
King's Cross Station.

156

7

From Coal Drops to New Train Shed

From Coal Drops to New Train Shed

.   .   . *'a row of brick and concrete coal drops'* which were erected by the Midland Railway in the nineteenth century. They were used for the storage of coal brought by the trains. From there the coal was distributed. They were rebuilt in the 1950s, their cavernous brick arches occupied by garages offering *'valeting and repairs'*.[1]

Many of the photographs in this section are here through the support of London and Continental Railways, who gave guidance over their site frequently between 2003 and 2006. Other photographs were taken off site.

Prominent above one of the coal drop arches was a ship's FIGUREHEAD on the east side of Pancras Road, just south of the Old St Pancras Church. The figurehead adorned a workshop called *'Long John Silver'* run by two ex-railwaymen making wooden toys, rocking chairs and rocking horses, all for sale. The advertisement for the 'body repair shop' immediately next door was apt for the grossly endowed figure who was certainly in need of some regeneration. She was a landmark, deliberately distasteful, and comic.

All of the coal drops in Pancras Road, and those in Midland Road were bulldozed to make way for the new railway lines and for the new train shed, a massive extension of the old Barlow Shed. The first part of this shed to be built was the eastern side. While this was being done the Midland trains ran on the old lines on the western side of the station. The last train out of the Barlow Shed on the western side was the 23.40 for Derby on Good Friday, April 9th, 2004.[2] On April 10th the Midland trains ran from the eastern side of the station where new railway track had been laid. The transfer was seamless. Trains travelled from the eastern side of the station until 17th July 2006 when they returned to the western side on new railway tracks, from where they now run on a permanent basis.

---

1. Camden History Society, Streets of St Pancras, Somers Town and the Railway Lands (page 102) published 2002

2. Ken Clench, railway enthusiast

Figurehead

May 2000

Ship's figurehead adorning a workshop called Long John Silver run by two ex-railwaymen. The Body Repair Centre was a garage next door.

167

1. Midland Train approaching
St Pancras Station
April 2004
Seen over old coal drops about to
be bulldozed. The eastern part of
the new station can be seen here.

2. Eastern Side of the
railway construction
October 2004
Coal drops on the right have now
been demolished to make way for the
western side of the new train shed.

1. Clearing Land
October 2003

This is another view of the Pancras Road coal drops about to be bulldozed.

2. Cleared Land
July 2004

Ready for the construction of the western side of St Pancras International.

Giraffes

March 2002

Construction on the new
St Pancras Gardens Wall.

Eastern Railway Site
October 2003
Making ready for new railway lines. The
Waterpoint can be seen in its new position.

New Platform and Train
Shed under construction
April 2003
Taken from the roof of the
Barlow Shed. The new
alignment of Camley Street
and Goods Way is
visible on the right.

View over King's Cross Central
April 2003
Stanley and Culross Buildings are on the
right and Gasholder 8 in the centre. Taken
from the roof of the Barlow Shed.

King's Cross St Pancras
Underground development
August 2004
View from Camden Council Offices in Argyle
Street looking across at King's Cross.

St Pancras Station
October 2004
Looking south from just below the Old St Pancras Church Gardens at the eastern side of the train shed roof.

172

1. Road Tunnel 1
November 2002
View from the western side showing old coal drops and new train bridge.

2. Road Tunnel 2
April 2004
Road runnning under the eastern side of the new train shed and old coal drops on the western side.

1. Road Tunnel 3
July 2004
Under the eastern part of the new train shed after removal of the western coal drops.

2. Road Tunnel 4
December 2006
The same road tunnel from the eastern side, this time under the completed train shed.

Coal Drops by Night
April 2004
Seen here on the western side of
the train shed used as road tunnels.

Framed 1

March 2004

Men working on eastern side
of the new train shed.

Framed 2
April 2004
Roof work on the eastern side
of the new train shed.

1. Crane 1
April 2003
Working on the new train shed roof. Seen from the roof of the Barlow Shed..

2. Eastern Roof, new Train Shed
September 2003
In its early stages seen from the new Pancras Road.

1. Crane 2
December 2005
Working on the western side
of the new train shed roof.

2. Roof 1
December 2005
During construction.

Roof 2

August 2005

Close up of the intricate work on the western side of the new train shed roof.

Re-roofing the Barlow Shed
December 2005

Contrasts 1
October 2004
Stanley Buildings North seen from
Culross Buildings Roof with St Pancras
Station and the Barlow Shed in the distance.

Contrasts 2

December 2005

Rooftop of the entrance to the St Pancras
Station, taken from the Barlow Shed with
the German Gymnasium. Stanley Buildings
and Gasholder 8 are in the distance.

1. Snake
April 2003
Old railway line coming into St Pancras Station and Pancras Road with the new road tunnel through the coal drops.

2. The old St Pancras Railway Bridge
April 2002

1. Pulling down the old
St Pancras Railway Bridge
June 2004

2. The last part of the
old Brill Bridge
October 2004

Working on the western side of the railway

June 2004

Western façade of King's Cross Station
and the Great Northern Hotel
August 2006
Showing work on the Northern Ticket Hall.

190

1. Roof of the
Great Northern Hotel
August 2004
Showing cranes working in close
proximity on the underground below.

2. Roof of King's Cross Station
April 2003
Showing the clock tower surrounded
by cranes working on the land at
the western side of the station.

Side by Side

September 2003

Early days building the new train shed roof on the eastern side of the station. It shows the close proximity of Stanley Buildings North now demolished.

8

New Railway Lines

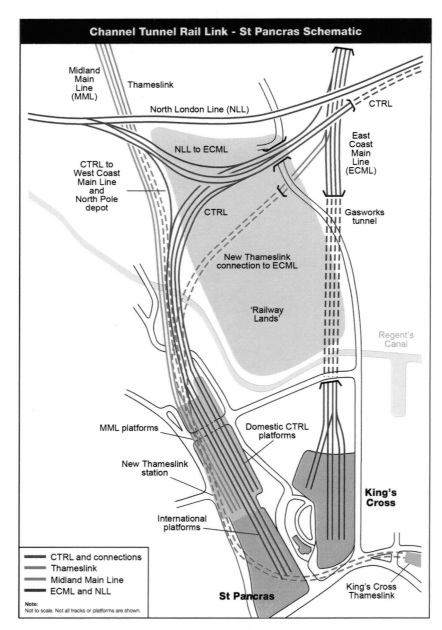

Channel Tunnel Rail Link - St Pancras Schematic

Midland Main Line (MML)

Thameslink

North London Line (NLL)

NLL to ECML

CTRL

CTRL to West Coast Main Line and North Pole depot

East Coast Main Line (ECML)

CTRL

Gasworks tunnel

New Thameslink connection to ECML

'Railway Lands'

Regent's Canal

MML platforms

Domestic CTRL platforms

New Thameslink station

King's Cross

International platforms

St Pancras

King's Cross Thameslink

CTRL and connections
Thameslink
Midland Main Line
ECML and NLL

Note:
Not to scale. Not all tracks or platforms are shown.

Map by kind permission of Union Railways (North) Ltd

Photograph one: NEW SLEEPERS October 2003: preliminary work for railway lines. Photograph two: WORK ON NEW RAILWAYS LINES March 2004: the track is almost ready for April 10th 2004, when the Midland Mainline service is transferred from the western side of the Barlow Shed to new lines on the east. In the next two photographs railwaymen are laying new rail tracks.

Despite these construction works to the new station from 2003-06 the Midland Mainline service continued to run seamlessly, at first from the west side of the Barlow Shed, then from the eastern side of the new train shed, and then once more on the western side but this time from the new train shed where it runs today.

'St. Pancras International will have 15 platforms: 6 for international Eurostar services, 3 for high-speed domestic services to Kent, 4 for Midland Mainline services to the East Midlands and Yorkshire and 2 below-ground for Thameslink cross-London services.' [1]

---

1. Channel Tunnel Rail Link – At a Glance pamphlet, produced by LCR

New sleepers
October 2003
Ready for the new track on the
eastern side of the station.

Work on new railway lines
March 2004
Eastern side of the station.

Teamwork

March 2004

Placing down the new lines on the
eastern side of the station.

Work on new track
February, 2006
The western side of the station just near
Old St Pancras Church.

9

Barlow Shed, Underground and Thameslink

THE BARLOW SHED

London and Continental Railways and Stonewest Ltd. permitted photographs to be taken on site. Great care, faithful to the original constructed between 1866-68, has been taken in restoration both inside and outside the building. Most of the *'2.5 acres of glass'* [1] in the Barlow roof had been *'destroyed in World War II'*. The glass has now been restored, as have the sky blue wrought-iron lattice arch ribs. Even on dull days the sky blue paint enlivens the soul. The white-painted finials on the roof near the apex are crafted meticulously.

THE UNDERGROUND

The first underground in the world was built between Paddington and Farringdon via King's Cross, the latter station being opened in 1863. The underground at King's Cross St Pancras, as it is now called, has undergone new development, which proceeded at the same time as the works on the new Channel Tunnel Terminal. The entrance to the underground into St Pancras from Euston Road is very impressive.

THAMESLINK

The Thameslink station at King's Cross is to be replaced with a station underneath St Pancras Station. This will mean a different route for commuters who until now have entered the station in Pentonville Road.

---

1. Camden History Society, Streets of St Pancras Somers Town and the Railway Lands, Published 2002 (page 105)

Work in the Barlow Shed
December 2005

Work in the Barlow Shed
July 2005

The Undercroft

July 2005

1. Thameslink Tunnel
March 2004
Revealed on western side of
St Pancras Station.

2. Work on new Thameslink Station
March 2004
Below the new train shed.

Thames Link underground work
October 2004

Restoration in progress
December 2005
Inside the Barlow Shed at the northern end.

Work on the Thameslink Box
March 2004

1. Old Barlow Roof
and chimneys
April 2003
Looking towards Euston Road
and Belgrove Street.

2. Barlow Roof
and new chimneys
July 2006
Process of restoration looking south towards
the St Pancras Chambers Clock Tower.

1. Barlow Roof looking south
Jully 2006
Showing the line of chimneys which are now to be used as part of the heating and cooling system of the building.

2. Barlow Roof looking north
Jully 2006
A complimentary view to photograph 2 on the opposite page looking northward.

Restoration of the
Barlow Arch
July 2006
Taken from Brill Place
showing the close proximity
of the new train shed.

216

Restored finials on the Barlow Roof
July 2006

1. Northern Arch of Barlow Roof
August 2006
Taken from inside the station.
Restoration almost completed.

2. Edge of the Terminal Roof
October 2006
Photographed from Pancras Road.

Renovated iron, stone and brick
April 2007
Detail of wrought iron lattice arch against
stone work inside the Barlow Shed.

Western Span
April 2007
Renovation inside the Barlow Shed.

Barlow Shed Roof
looking north
July 2006
Showing the glorious sky blue
finish to the metal work.
Restoration in progress.

10

Camley Street Natural Park

Camley Street Natural Park was created alongside the Regent's Canal in 1983. The site was originally a coal drop for the Great Northern Railway. Before this date a group of local people found orchids growing by the canal. Ken Livingstone, then Head of the Greater London Council, supported children, parents and teachers as they built and landscaped a wildlife park. It was opened as a London Wildlife Trust[1] nature reserve in 1985.

The natural park is a haven where the presence of birds, wild flowers, trees, pond and canal so fill the mind that the noise of construction and traffic recede from consciousness, and images of industry – first the gasholders and later the cranes – are softened as the pond reflects them. The park is loved by visitors, volunteers and workers from the Wildlife Trust. The Regent's Canal with its barges, the tow-path with its cyclists and walkers, the nearby Coal and Fish Offices (1852), weathered by time since their construction, all add colour and variety to the scene.

How the function of this park may be affected by the new King's Cross Central Development is a vital concern. The hut where adults and children learn about nature is to be replaced. A bridge is planned over one end of the park for walkers and cyclists. Only the future will tell how the park survives. It may be for the better, it may not.

---

1. 'London Wildlife Trust is one of 47 Wildlife Trusts which together form a nationwide network of local nature conservation charities. They take action to protect the UK's natural world. Collectively the Wildlife Trusts care for almost 2,500 nature reserves. The partnership campaigns for the protection of wildlife and invests in the future by helping people of all ages gain a greater understanding of nature.' (London Wildlife Trust statement)

CAMLEY STREET NATURAL PARK LATE SUMMER

Reedmace rustle in the wind, their chocolate
heads like cut-out fingers against speared leaves.
Convolvulus along the pond's embankment
trumpets its white flowers against the green.
Purple loosestrife runs wild, seducing bees.
A speckled wood butterfly, velvet brown,
wings spread out, lies sleepily on burdock,
its eyespots winking in the light.

                    Mint grows
in a watery bed.

                    Above its head
a dragonfly, blue brilliance,
                         jerks here and there.

Alders rise above the park, their branches
like brushes waving at the water life,
greening the Coal and Fish Offices, sea of
brick,
      sculpted curve moving gracefully
away,
      crack willow emeralds the grey.

By the canal a duckling stretches, flops,
adjusts its wobbly legs.

         A coot midstream
sits on a floating nest, and from the reeds
a heron takes to the air, flap flapping towards
its prey.

      On the towpath cyclists weave
their wheels between the walkers and the dogs.
Canal boats cast their colours through the hedge
while water gushes in the lock.

Angela Inglis

Reedmace
Movember 2005
A scene in central London.
From the northern end of
Camley Street Natural Park.

Narrowboat at St Pancras Lock
April 2004
Showing the way in which the gasholder
and other buildings compliment the scene.

1. The Seahorse
April 2004
Home to a family on the Regent's Canal. St Pancras Station can be seen in the background.

2. Regent's Canal
June 2005
Seen from Camley Street Park glimpsing the barge Mr. Micawber, two narrowboats and a runner on the towpath.

1. Nettle Leaved Bellflower, Camley Street Natural Park
2. Lesser Periwinkle, waste ground at side of Goods Way
3. Nodding Bur-marigold, waste ground at the side of Goods Way
4. Tulips in Old St Pancras Gardens
5. Giant Hogweed, Camley Street Natural Park
6. Norfolk Reeds Camley Street Natural Park
7. Teasel, Camley Street Natural Park
8. Oxey Daisies and Poppies in waste ground below Gasholder 8
9. Honeysuckle on Camley Street Natural Park fence

1. Norfolk Reeds Autumn, Camley Street Natural Park
2. Oxeye Daisies in waste ground
3. Honeysuckle Berries, Camley Street Natural Park

4. Evening Primrose, waste ground below Gasholder 8
5. Giant Hogweed, Camley Street Natural Park
6. Old Man's Beard, Camley Street Natural Park

7. Hollyhocks, Canal Boat, Regent's Canal at the side of Camley Street Natural Park
8. Lesser Periwinkle, waste ground at side of Goods Way
9. Thistles in waste ground below Gasholder 8

1. Summer Reflections
Summer 1997
Five gasholders reflected in
the large pond.

2. Winter Reflections
February 1997
Reflection in the small pond.

236

1. Coal and Fish Offices
April 2005
Seen from Camley Street Natural Park
Built 1852 beside the Regent's Canal.

2. Coal and Fish Offices
with Norfolk Reeds
November 2005
From Camley Street Natural Park.

Sunset

December 2005

Side view of the Coal and Fish Offices from Goods Way. They are built at the side of the canal. Constructed in several phases from 1852. These industrial brick buildings have been repaired and will have a new life as part of the King's Cross Central development.

1. Working crane
January 2004
Reflection in big pond.

2. Crane dismantled
March 2004
Reflection in big pond.

1. Crane One
January 2004
Reflection in big pond.

2. Crane Two
March 2004
Reflection in big pond.

Snow Scene
February 2004
Camley Street Natural Park
photographed from the southern
end. The wooden hut is the
educational centre for the park.

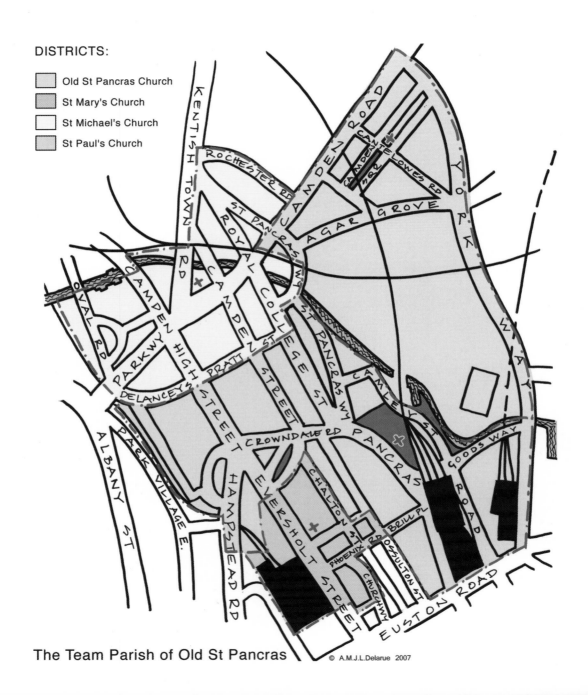

The Team Parish of Old St Pancras

© A.M.J.L.Delarue 2007

Appendix

APPENDIX 1

'Originally the church stood just above the flood bank of the River Fleet, on an ancient track connecting the City of London to what is now Hampstead Road. From the ninth century the parish stretched from Ken Wood in the north, down to the next parish of St Giles in the Fields at an important crossing of the Roman Road now called Oxford Street',[1] and from what is now Regent's Park in the west to the present York Way in the East, boundaries which encompass much of the current London Borough of Camden. Today Old St Pancras Church is one of four in the new Parish of Old St Pancras which has existed only since 2003. The parishes of St Pancras, St Mary's Somers Town, St Michael's Camden Town and St Paul's Camden Square comprise the Team Parish of Old St Pancras Church *(see map).*

---

1. Pamplet, Mission Action Plan 2004 to 2008 The District of St Pancras Old Church in the parish of Old St Pancras

APPENDIX 2

There were two graveyards in the vicinity, the St Pancras graveyard around the church, on which Hardy worked, and St Giles graveyard on the northern side of the church, close to St Pancras Hospital which was once the workhouse.[1] According to Malcolm Holmes, the Borough Archivist, and according to Walter Brown[2], the tombstones around the tree come from St. Giles Graveyard, in which Hardy did not work, so the name "Hardy Tree" is misleading. Both St Giles and the St Pancras Burial Grounds were closed in 1854 because of overcrowding and unsanitary conditions. They were opened as gardens in 1877. As a burial ground it had the reputation that *'excluding Westminster Abbey there is no other parish in England that can claim to be the 'last resting place' for so many celebrated personages as St Pancras'.* [3]

---

1. Walter E. Brown, St Pancras Open Spaces and Disused Burial Grounds, Town Hall, Pancras Road, Camden Town, London, 1911

2. As above (page 2)

3. As above (page 3)

APPENDIX 3

HISTORY OF THE LAND THAT USED TO BE THE COAL DROPS

It is hard to believe that in the eighteenth century where the railway and new station are now situated on the site of the demolished coal drops there were avenues of trees. From the Streets of St Pancras[1] we learn that it was a fashionable spa, Pancras Wells, *'one of several along the banks of the River Fleet or 'River of Wells'. In 1700, its two pump-rooms offered a choice of purgative chalybeate water for 3 pence a day or half a guinea for the whole season. Stretching southwards as far as far as Goods Way were extensive garden walks shaded by avenues of trees. By 1722 the spa's reputation had declined – there were complaints about "scandalous company" and dancing - but by 1769 the Wells had seemingly recovered its good name.'[1]*

We then read that *'The spa had closed by 1797, when a map shows the first houses built over its gardens. These were picturesque Church Hill, which climbed gently eastward (overlooking the churchyard). After 1800 it then continued southward as Essex Place and, eventually, Spann's Buildings (a local centre of clay pipe manufacture). Linking the latter to the main road were diminutive Dorset Place and King's Place. Facing what is now Pancras Road were Church Terrace and further south, Church Row.'[2]*

Appendix

We also learn that Sir Henry Bessemer lived here in Baxter House from 1841 to 1862 and that *'in a small factory erected in the back garden he manufactured his famed 'bronze powder' an inexpensive substitute for the 'gold powder'.*[3] *He was the man who patented a 'celebrated Bessemer Converter whereby steel could at last be cheaply manufactured by blowing air through molten pig-iron to remove the impurities.'*[4]

All these little streets and houses were swept away for the building of the coal drops. Walter Brown writes about St Pancras Old Churchyard and the area surrounding it that, *'No part of London or its neighbourhood has ever undergone such rapid and extensive transformation in such a short time as this portion of St Pancras, hundreds of houses being demolished to make room for the extensions of the railway.'*[5]

1. Camden History Society, Streets of St. Pancras, Somers Town and the Railway Lands 2002 (page 102)

2. As above

3. As above

4. As above

5. Walter E. Brown, St Pancras Open Spaces and Disused Burial Grounds, Town Hall, Pancras Road, Camden Town, London, 1911 (page 7)

Bibliography

Camden History Society, *Streets of St Pancras, Somers Town and the Railway Lands,* published by Camden History Society, 2002.

Walter E. Brown, *St Pancras Open Spaces and Disused Burial Grounds,* published by Town Hall, Pancras Road, Camden Town, London, 1911.

MAGAZINES

Robert Leon, Article *The Man who made King's Cross,* Camden History Review 17.

Germaine Greer, Article *Cornerstone,* SPAB News, Volume 24, Number 4, 2003, page 64.

PAMPHLETS

The District of St Pancras Old Church in the parish of Old St Pancras. Mission Action Plan, 2004 to 2008.

The St Pancras Waterpoint. Available at the Waterpoint, St Pancras Yacht Basin, Camley Street, King's Cross, London NW1.

Channel Tunnel Rail Link - At a Glance 2005-06. LCR pamphlet.

TALK

Malcolm Holmes, up to February 2007, Senior Archivist, Camden Local Studies and Archives, *Talk on St Pancras Chambers.*

Acknowledgements

Father Bruce Batstone, Old St Pancras Church

Del Brenner

Pat Clough, Photographer and Teacher

Graham Crostan, Tony Holland and Ray Yates

Anthony Delarue, Architect

Michael Edwards, Bartlett School of Architecture

Professor Germaine Greer

Peter Herbert, Exhibitions Manager, St Pancras Hospital

Rob Inglis

Werner Kienberger, Bella 2 Café

Judith Martin, Projects Organiser, Industrial Buildings Preservation Trust

Dinesh Patel

Robin Stummer. Editor, Cornerstone

Jeanne Thomason and Ken Clench

Hilary Vernon Smith, Head Scenic Artist, Royal National Theatre, London.

Richard Knight, Principal Officer, Camden Local Studies and Archives and staff

Malcolm Holmes, Senior Archivist, Camden Local Studies and Archives

The Department of Culture and Environment, London Borough of Camden

Camden History Society
Staff at Camley Street Natural Park
London Wildlife Trust
Photo Books International, London
Staff at the Channel Tunnel Rail Link project:
      London & Continental Railways
      Union Railways
      Rail Link Engineering
      CORBER (Costain O'Rourke Bachy Emcor Rail)
      London & Continental Stations & Property
Excel
Midland Mainline Ltd
Donovan Pauly, Stonewest Ltd
Future Events
Argent (King's Cross) Ltd
The Brunswick/Allied London Ltd
Goin Green, retailers of G Whiz electric cars

Biographies

Angela Inglis has been a resident of Kings Cross and St Pancras since 1986. While Head of English at a local comprehensive school she studied photography under the guidance of Pat Clough.

Her love and involvement with the area of King's Cross and St Pancras coincided with her passion for photography. This occurred when it became evident that the local landscape was to undergo a massive change. Angela set about developing an impressive archive of photographic images recording the local landscape. This produced requests from interested bodies which have resulted in numerous photographic exhibitions.

She has also been awarded five prizes in photographic competitions, staged by the Hampstead and Highgate Express, for her portrait and landscape work.

Web site: angelainglis.org

Nigel Buckner is a freelance designer and teacher of web, graphics and digital photo editing.

His work began in the pre-digital age and has involved a range of complimentary disciplines such as fine art, music, publicity, screen printing and t-shirt design.

He is based in London.

Web site: nigelbuckner.com